Dedication:

To the little dreamers, the budding artists, and the magic-weavers,

"Colorful Adventures Await!"

This coloring book is dedicated to you—the ones who turn blank pages into vibrant worlds. May your imagination soar like a kite caught in a playful breeze.

As you fill these pages with hues, remember that each stroke is a whisper to the universe. You're not just coloring; you're creating joy, one crayon at a time.

So here's to laughter, to wild imaginations, and to the delightful messiness of creativity. May your days be as bright as the sunniest yellow and as cozy as a bear's hug.

With love and endless possibilities,

Your fellow adventurer

P.S. Don't forget to color outside the lines—it's where the magic happens!

This book belongs to:

____

Araucária Publications

Test color page